CH00826105

Ben Youssef Mosque
After Koutoubia (see p010), tł
mosque is the second tallest i
which is unnervingly flat and ꞇ
when viewed from above. Named after an
Almoravid sultan, it was rebuilt several times
by succeeding dynasties. Its wooden crown
points the way to the *medersa* (see p034).
Off rue Souk El Khemis

Musée de Marrakech
Part of the lure of the Musée de Marrakech,
which exhibits Moroccan artefacts, is the
building – the 19th-century Dar Menebhi, a
beautifully restored Andalusian-style palace.
Place Ben Youssef, T 05 24 44 18 93

Sidi Ben Salah Zaouia
This particular *zaouia* (sanctuary) was built by
the Marinids, the Berber tribe that followed
hot on the heels of the Almohads and claimed
the city in 1269. It is easily distinguished by
its intricate 14th-century minaret.
Rue Ba Hmad

Sidi Bel Abbès Zaouia
In the north of the medina is a tranquil and
less touristy quarter named after the patron
saint of Marrakech, whose shrine is set within
an impressive *zaouia* and garden complex.
Jnane Sidi Bel Abbès

Souk El Khemis
For the patient, dedicated shopper, El Khemis
is the most interesting souk. All manner of
antiques, bric-a-brac and curios are hawked
in the stalls and daily outdoor market.
Off route des Remparts

INTRODUCTION
THE CHANGING FACE OF THE URBAN SCENE

'It's the most lovely spot in the world,' said Churchill to Roosevelt, as they gazed out over the Red City in 1943. Since its founding in the 11th century, this place has seduced visitors, from the craftsmen who built its mosques and palaces to the bohemians who rode the Marrakech Express at full throttle in the 1960s and 1970s, and the European politicians and US starlets who followed. Lately, it has grown up, emerging as one of the most sophisticated destinations in Africa. And while quick-fix Marrakech is more than willing to offer up its beguiling souks and mesmerising interior architecture to e-ticket tourists in search of winter sun and instant escapism, it has also become a player on the film and music festival circuit, a bona fide cultural heavyweight. The contemporary art and design scenes are flourishing as foreign creatives trade their New York or Paris studios for the 'Kech, and the number of locals launching their own businesses, from *boîtes* to boutiques, is on the rise.

After the French arrived in 1912, the city found a way to balance the ancient and the modern. Arguably, this is what makes it so alluring. If Morocco is the most liberal Arab country, Marrakech is its *ne plus ultra*. Another factor is glamour. You will find some of the most luxurious and romantic accommodation in the world, in one of the prettiest settings. Orientalist fantasy palace, intimate riad, impeccable five-star resort – it's all here. Classic Marrakech will always dazzle, but it has a fresh, 21st-century face too.

ESSENTIAL INFO

FACTS, FIGURES AND USEFUL ADDRESSES

TOURIST OFFICE

Office National Marocain du Tourisme
Place Abdel Moumen
Avenue Mohammed V
T 05 24 43 61 31
www.muchmorocco.com

TRANSPORT

Car hire
Avis
T 05 24 43 31 69
Hertz
T 05 24 44 72 39

Taxis
Petits taxis (small khaki-coloured Fiats,
Simcas or similar) can be flagged down
in the street. *Grands taxis* (larger cars,
normally Mercedes) are available for
longer distances and can be hired at the
railway station, most of the larger hotels
and cab ranks across the city

EMERGENCY SERVICES

Ambulance/Fire
T 150
Police
T 190
Pharmacy
Pharmacie Laboratoire Liberté
Place de la Liberté
T 05 24 44 69 51

CONSULATES

British Honorary Consulate
Avenue Abdelkrim El Khattabi
T 05 37 63 33 33
www.gov.uk/government/world/morocco
US Consulate General
8 boulevard Moulay Youssef
Casablanca
T 05 22 64 20 99
morocco.usembassy.gov

POSTAL SERVICES

Post office
Place du 16 Novembre/
Avenue Mohammed V
Shipping
UPS
T 05 37 77 62 22
www.ups.com

BOOKS

The Last Storytellers by Richard
Hamilton (IB Tauris)
**Marrakech: Living on the Edge of the
Desert** by Massimo Listri and Daniel Rey
(Images Publishing Group)
Marrakesh: Through Writers' Eyes
edited by Barnaby Rogerson and Rose
Baring (Eland Books)

WEBSITE

News
www.lemag.ma

EVENTS

Marrakech Art Fair
www.marrakechartfair.com
Marrakech Biennale
www.marrakechbiennale.org
Marrakech International Film Festival
www.festivalmarrakech.info

COST OF LIVING

Taxi from Menara Airport to city centre
120 dirhams
Cappuccino
30 dirhams
Packet of cigarettes
32 dirhams
Daily newspaper
4 dirhams
Bottle of champagne
1,200 dirhams

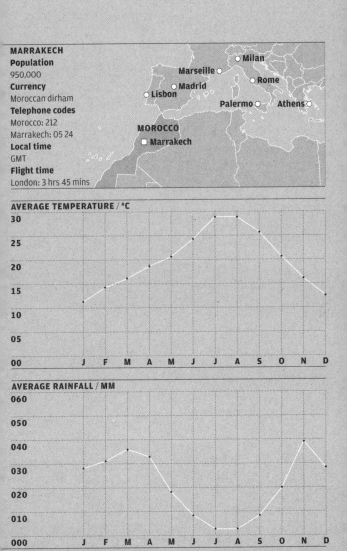

MARRAKECH
Population
950,000
Currency
Moroccan dirham
Telephone codes
Morocco: 212
Marrakech: 05 24
Local time
GMT
Flight time
London: 3 hrs 45 mins

MOROCCO
□ Marrakech

○ Milan
○ Marseille
○ Rome
○ Madrid
○ Lisbon
○ Palermo
○ Athens

AVERAGE TEMPERATURE / °C

	J	F	M	A	M	J	J	A	S	O	N	D
30
25
20
15
10
05
00

AVERAGE RAINFALL / MM

	J	F	M	A	M	J	J	A	S	O	N	D
060
050
040
030
020
010
000

NEIGHBOURHOODS

THE AREAS YOU NEED TO KNOW AND WHY

To help you navigate the city, we've chosen the most interesting districts (see below and the map inside the back cover) and colour-coded our featured venues, according to their location; those venues that are outside these areas are not coloured.

SOUTH MEDINA

Shaped like an arrowhead, Marrakech's medina is one of Africa's largest. Frenetic and wholly stimulating, the southern half is the busiest part. Enter via the boulevard that stems from Koutoubia Mosque (see p010) and use Place Jemaa El Fna as your reference point. Taxis are barred from the core and from the square after dark; pick one up at one of the gates. La Mamounia (see p026) offers respite from the chaos.

PALMERAIE

Legend has it this oasis was established in the 11th century by Youssef Ibn Tachfine, founder of Marrakech. Having made camp here, the sultan's servants spat out date seeds, thus planting the 200,000 or so palms growing in the area. Although much of the investment in luxury properties is now focused around Route de l'Ourika and Route d'Amizmiz, the Palmeraie still boasts some of the city's most appealing retreats, such as Palais Namaskar (see p022).

NORTH MEDINA

The heart of the old city is where most of the big tourist attractions lie: the souks, Ben Youssef complex (see p034) and Musée de Marrakech (place Ben Youssef, T 05 24 44 18 93). Less well trodden is the northern tip, where you'll spy workshops, bakeries, women on their way to the hammam, and other glimpses of urban life in an archaic setting. The market held around Souk El Khemis is worth a trawl.

HIVERNAGE

This leafy district of the new town is where the embassies of the French Protectorate and its officials set up home. Many of their descendants still live here, alongside green spaces including the Menara Gardens (see p014). Those who know Hivernage of old would barely recognise it today, due to the number of hip hotels and nightspots, such as The Pearl (see p016) and Epicurien (rue Ibrahim El Mazini, T 06 63 05 57 04).

MELLAH/KASBAH

At the 'base' of the arrowhead is the most ancient part of Marrakech, the Kasbah, and the former Jewish quarter of the Mellah, which dates back to the 16th century. Stay at Villa Makassar (see p020) and visit the remarkable Saadian Tombs (see p078) and the ruins of Palais El Badi (see p040). The architecture of the Mellah is distinct, its colourful facades and Spanish hanging balconies a legacy of the Moors and the Sephardic Jews who fled the Inquisition.

GUÉLIZ

The French Protectorate was described as 'soft colonialism': its urban planning aimed to create a homogeneous whole between the new town and the medina. The *ville nouvelle*'s art deco glory days have long passed, but today the district is buzzing once again. Stroll along its wide avenues, visiting the streetside cafés and shops. Venues like Kechmara (see p053) and Azar (see p054) inject vigour into the nightlife.

LANDMARKS

THE SHAPE OF THE CITY SKYLINE

In the labyrinth of medieval Marrakech, defining landmarks are hard to identify. One exception is Koutoubia Mosque (overleaf), whose minaret dominates the skyline and acts as a gateway to the old city's sprawling morphology. The medina itself is ringed by 10km of ramparts (see p012), with ornamental entrances (*babs*) that give their names to its neighbourhoods and hubs. The focal point is Place Jemaa El Fna, the huge square that you'll return to again and again as you navigate this part of town; its night market is a spectacle you should view at least once. From here, the souks lie to the north, and the Palais El Badi (see p040) and Saadian Tombs (see p078) to the south. Both are within walking distance.

The peaceful Menara Gardens (see p014), about 3km from the city centre, are a world away from the medina. Journey through Hivernage and the landscape changes quickly from leafy urban streets lined with modern apartment blocks to vast olive groves. Head north into Guéliz, the heart of the *ville nouvelle*, and the scenery shifts again; Jardin Majorelle (see p036) is a reminder of the once-gracious cityscape of the French Protectorate. Sadly, most of Marrakech's art deco architecture is gone, although the 1923 La Mamounia (see p026), a legendary grande dame, still stands. It is perhaps the city's best-loved landmark, and its dusky pink walls and famous gardens continue to impress due to a major restoration. *For full addresses, see Resources.*

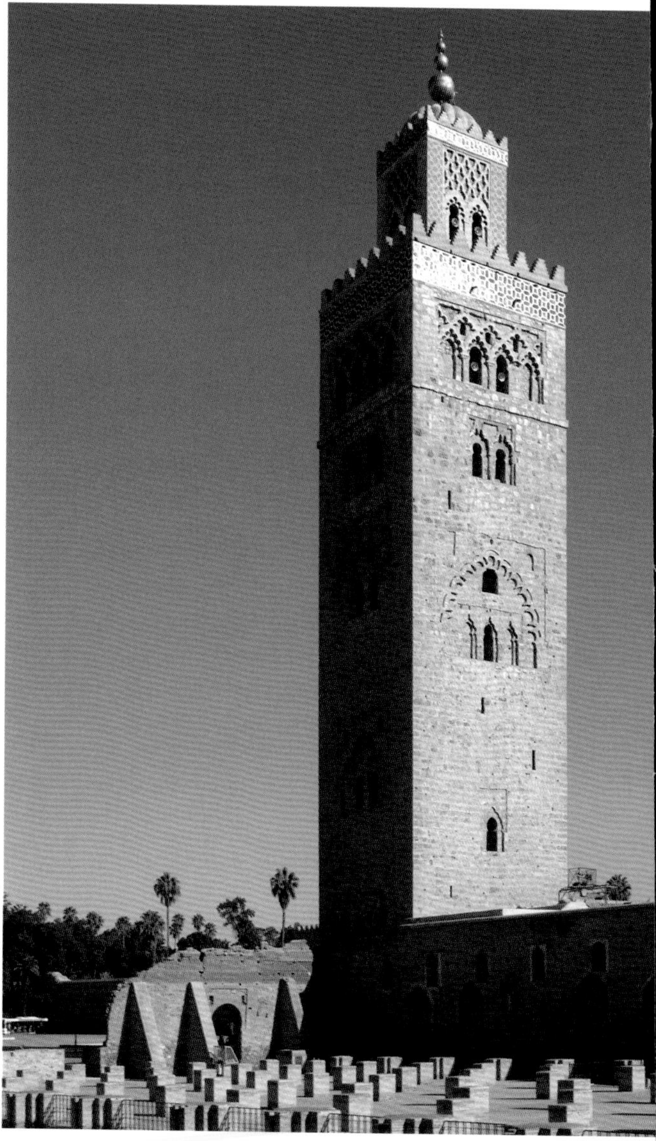

Koutoubia Mosque

The Almohads completed Koutoubia's 69m minaret in 1189 and its proportions became standard for others throughout Morocco. This was their second chance to get it right; the first minaret had to be torn down because its orientation towards Mecca was askew. Koutoubia was built on the site of an existing Almoravid mosque, and its name derives from the Arabic word *koutoubiyyin* (librarian); bookstalls were once set up around its base. As with most mosques in the Arab world, non-Muslims are barred from entering and will have to imagine the interior. The tower has six rooms, one on top of the other, and the exterior features the horseshoe-shaped arches that are typical of the Andalusian-influenced Almohad style. During the five daily prayer sessions, the faithful file in from the serene surrounding gardens.
Avenue Mohammed V

Ramparts

Remarkably intact, the mud-and-lime wall that encloses the medina has borne witness to numerous sieges (the city was conquered by various colonising powers before it came under French rule in 1912). Of its main gates, Bab Agnaou and Bab Er Rob are the most interesting. Route des Remparts, which runs along the medina's eastern flank, provides the best vantage point to appreciate the scale and expanse.

Menara Gardens
Echoes of these 12th-century gardens can
be glimpsed throughout Marrakech. The
outdoor pool at La Mamounia (see p026)
took its inspiration from Menara's central
reservoir, and its pioneering irrigation
system, responsible for watering what are
some of the oldest gardens in Morocco,
has been replicated all across the country
and in Spain. Menara was the vision of
Almohad ruler Abd Al-Mu'min, who sought
to provide his citizens with a manmade
oasis around which they could grow crops
and escape from the heat. With the Atlas
Mountains forming a stunning backdrop,
the gardens have been a popular (and
romantic) sanctuary for Marrakechis ever
since. The focal point is a 19th-century
pavilion (right), which replaced a 16th-
century structure built by the Saadians.
Open daily from 8am to 7pm.
Avenue de la Ménara

HOTELS

WHERE TO STAY AND WHICH ROOMS TO BOOK

Since the 1990s, riads and the smaller *dars* (traditional courtyard houses) have been snapped up by foreigners and converted into high-spec *maisons d'hôte*, and Marrakech now has a dizzying array of accommodation – but do be choosy, as a zellige-tiled bathroom will do little to compensate for low water pressure. In the medina, Riad de Tarabel (8 derb Sraghna, T 05 24 39 17 06) is a stylish riff on the colonial, and the white-on-white aesthetic of Riad Elisa (21 rue Sidi El Yamani, T 06 00 06 70 67) sets it apart. El Fenn (2 derb Moullay Abdullah Ben Hezzian, T 05 24 44 12 10) is the jetsetters' choice, popular for its eclectic interior, superlative service and art stash. Impressive budget options are P'tit Habibi (59 bis Zaouia Sidi Bellabes, T 05 24 37 88 87), which blends Nordic simplicity and midcentury furniture, and Riad Goloboy (derb Mbarek, T 06 61 23 03 05), where pop art and graffiti meld with arabesque arches.

Guéliz and Hivernage offer contemporary properties, such as The Pearl (avenue Echouhada, T 05 24 42 42 42) and Bab Hotel (angle boulevard Mansour Eddahbi, T 05 24 43 52 50). You'll find the secluded oases Dar Sabra (Douar Abiad, T 05 24 32 91 72) and Palais Namaskar (see p022) in Palmeraie, and for a bucolic setting to boot, head to the outskirts and the revived Amanjena (route de Ouarzazate km12, T 05 24 39 90 00), the Selman (route d'Amizmiz km5, T 05 24 45 96 00) or the Mandarin Oriental (see p018).
For full addresses and room rates, see Resources.

Riad Mena

A serene bolthole tucked behind Jemaa El Fna, Riad Mena is elegantly hip. Owner Philomena Schurer Merckoll and designer Romain Michel Menière overhauled and consolidated two neighbouring properties over a seven-year period. Interiors feature polished plaster floors and pale terracotta *bejmat* (floor tiles), offset by bold-hued furnishings, such as the gleaming black Eero Saarinen table in the dining space,

and a red Arne Jacobsen 'Egg' seat in the lounge. Original elements, like the domed ceiling in the Eileen Gray suite, have been meticulously restored; the simple, stylish Traveller suite (above) benefits from a big tub. There is also a good-sized lap pool and a spacious rooftop, which is shaded by textiles from Marrakshi Life (see p090). *70 derb Jdid, T 05 24 38 18 28, www.riadmenaandbeyond.com*

Mandarin Oriental

The MO joined the luxury-brand invasion in 2015. Its polished, airy interiors are by Gilles & Boissier, and the seven Atlas Suites have wide terraces with plunge pools; elsewhere, the lavish spa decor (pictured) was inspired by Córdoba's Mezquita. At dinner, head to Hakkasan's happening sister restaurant Ling Ling for shared plates and killer cocktails.
Route Golf Royal, T 05 24 29 88 88

Villa Makassar

Fouad Graidia spent five years restoring and embellishing two Kasbah houses, turning one into this handsome hotel. Inside, he has displayed the assortment of art deco and modernist furniture and objects that he's been collecting since 1998. The library is a fine case in point, featuring Bauhaus-style onyx (similar to that used for dividing walls in the Mies van der Rohe Pavilion in Barcelona), chaises longues by Le Corbusier and lamps by Jean Perzel. The most striking of Villa Makassar's 10 unique rooms are the Suite Grand Luxe Double (pictured) and the Mondrian-inspired Standard. Unusually for the medina, the property has indoor and outdoor pools, as well as an atmospheric spa and hammam. *20 derb Chtouka, T 05 24 39 19 26, www.villamakassar.com*

Palais Namaskar

The Arab genius for using reflecting pools
as a cooling feature in landscaped gardens
comes into play in Philippe Soulier's chic
resort, which he devised in conjunction
with the Franco-Algerian architect Imaad
Rahmouni. Operated by Oetker Collection,
Palais Namaskar is a lavish but modern
take on the Moorish aesthetic; its private
accommodations, like the one-bedroom
Pool Villa (above and opposite), are tucked
within attractive walled gardens. Daybeds
and rope hammocks are scattered across
the manicured lawns. There's a sumptuous
restaurant, whose design incorporates a
gold mirrored bar and ornate Murano glass
chandeliers. Moroccan-influenced French
cuisine by chef Antoine Perray – seabass
carpaccio with saffron, for example – and
sensational Atlas Mountain views from the
rooftop bar add to its many merits.
88/69 route de Bab Atlas, T 05 24 29 98 00,
www.palaisnamaskar.com

Peacock Pavilions

Set in an olive grove 20 minutes' drive from Marrakech, Peacock Pavilions was established by American husband-and-wife team Chris and Maryam Montague in 2011. Here, they have conceived three light-filled, contemporary riads, bursting with eclectic furniture and objets d'art, like Frank Gehry's corrugated cardboard 'Wiggle Side Chair' and an ornate Afghani camel bridle. The tribal-chic Atlas Pavilion (above) draws inspiration from Jeanne Lanvin's apartment in Paris. The property doubles as a centre for the couple's NGO Project SOAR, whose remit is to keep girls in school. Yoga is high on the agenda, and the vegetarian dishes are superlative, yet an outdoor cinema and a lovely pool with a stylish cabana make for a playful vibe. *Route de Ouarzazate km18, T 05 24 48 46 17, www.peacockpavilions.com*

Riad Dixneuf la Ksour

Designed by Studio KO, who also revamped Le Grand Café de la Poste (see p032), Riad Dixneuf packs quite a punch. The entrance plunges straight into a pale-pink marble-lined courtyard, dug down in order to allow the columns to soar and lend a sense of height and grandeur. A gold-and-green mosaicked ornamental pool and cane patio furniture hint at old-fashioned glamour; and wraparound balconies offer vantage points from which to drink it in. Situated up a sinuous staircase are six spacious rooms (Medersa Suite, above). All but the Tanger Room, a nook for lone travellers, have fireplaces, desks and reading chairs. If you don't fancy facing the fray, just stay in for an excellent home-cooked Moroccan meal in the wood-panelled Africa lounge. *19 rue Sidi El Yamani, T 05 24 38 41 32, www.dixneuf-la-ksour.com*

La Mamounia
Interior designer Jacques Garcia, aided by
an army of artisans, brought contemporary
glamour to this storied hotel following a
scrupulous renovation. Several years on,
the allure of La Mamounia and its unique
ambience remains undiminished. Rooms
are opulent, the spa (pictured) exquisite
and the celebrated gardens enchanting.
Avenue Bab Jdid, T 05 24 38 86 00,
www.mamounia.com

Dar Kawa

Buried deep in a knot of streets close to the Ben Youssef complex (see p034) and Musée de Marrakech (T 05 24 44 18 93), Dar Kawa's difficult-to-find location may seem daunting. However, if you want to feel the beating pulse of the medina, few addresses beat it. Opened in 2011, the riad is a collaboration between Belgian textile designer Valérie Barkowski and architect Quentin Wilbaux, who helped restore the 17th-century Saadian house. In a city infused with colour, the pale slate-hued zellige and dove-grey woodwork in the courtyard (above) are refreshing. Of the four rooms, we plumped for the Olmassi Suite, for its appliqué rug and African furniture. On the roof terrace, escape the afternoon heat on an antique day bed.
18 derb El Ouali, Kaat Ben Nahed,
T 06 61 34 43 33, www.darkawa.net

Riad Due

Finding a riad with a contemporary decor is not very hard these days, but the two properties (Riad Due and Riad 72) run by Italian photographer-turned-hotelier Giovanna Cinel remain standouts. In the four-room Due, modern furniture has been melded with Berber carpets and pieces by Marrakechi artisans and artists; in its Zan Suite (above), you'll find a decorative hand-beaten copper bath, sourced from Yahya Création (see p068). Cinel's design nous can be seen everywhere, from the revamped art deco chairs flanking the teal-coloured plunge pool to ram-horn hooks in the bathrooms. The landscaping is also a highlight, with artful planting in the courtyard and on the roof. The terrace at Riad 72 is particularly pretty.
2 derb Chentouf, T 05 24 38 76 29, www.riadliving.com

Fellah Hotel
A 15-minute drive from town, this hotel
exudes tranquillity. It adjoins and helps
fund the non-profit Dar Al-Ma'mûn arts
centre, established in 2010. Ten villas
house 69 rooms, such as the chic Suite
103 (pictured), and interiors feature local
rugs and leatherwork. The scenic pool is
a draw, as is the restaurant, which uses
produce grown in Fellah's gardens.
Route de l'Ourika km13, T 05 25 06 50 00

24 HOURS

SEE THE BEST OF THE CITY IN JUST ONE DAY

Marrakech throws up myriad moments: stumbling across an age-old bakery or catching the scents of the spice souk as you wander through the medina are experiences that will make your visit. The best way to discover the old city is to just dive in at the epicentre, Jemaa El Fna. Mornings are the square's down time. After dark, it is a frenzy of merchants, musicians and soothsayers. Brasserie-style Le Salama (40 rue des Banques, T 05 24 39 13 00) is a blingy stop-off for a bite to eat or a drink. The souks (see p080) are the area's main attraction, but can be a tourist trap. A subtler introduction to historical local culture is Maison de la Photographie (opposite).

Aside from the itinerary detailed here, you could spend the day exploring the contemporary art scene (see p064), perhaps starting at Musée de la Palmeraie (Dar Tounsi, route de Fès, T 06 10 40 80 96), which has a beautiful setting. Another long-time favourite is concept store 33 rue Majorelle (33 rue Yves Saint-Laurent, T 05 24 31 41 95), for its keen edit of local product design and fashion.

Bar and club culture is somewhat underwhelming, but there are exceptions, particularly around the new town: Le Salon at Le Grand Café de la Poste (place du 16 Novembre, T 05 24 43 30 38) is an institution, and Bar Marocain, set inside La Mamounia (see p026), serves a top-notch martini. You will find international DJs at superclub Theatro (rue Ibrahim El Mazini, T 06 64 86 03 39). *For full addresses, see Resources.*

09.30 Maison de la Photographie

This peaceful courtyard gallery offers a great introduction to Moroccan history. Its owners, Patrick Manac'h and Hamid Mergani, bought the medina property to house their private collection of vintage photographs, which includes more than 10,000 unique images. The exhibition is displayed chronologically over several floors, beginning downstairs with photos of Tangier taken in the late 19th century.

Also on show here is the first colour film of Berber culture, made by Daniel Chicault in 1957. Linger on the roof terrace for fresh juice and views of the old city. In the village of Tafza, 35 minutes' drive from Marrakech, Manac'h and Mergani have established the Ecomusée Berbère de l'Ourika (T 05 24 38 57 21), focusing on rural life and crafts. *46 rue Ahal Fès, T 05 24 38 57 21, www.maisondelaphotographie.ma*

11.00 Ben Youssef Medersa

Nowhere in the city is the influence of the
Andalusian style as evident as within this
medersa. The structure's origins date to
the 14th century but it was then rebuilt by
the Saadians in 1565, when Marrakech's
medersas were considered great centres
of learning and gold-rich sultans threw
their abundant assets into the rundown
city. This remained a functioning school
until 1960, and it opened to the public
in 1982. After passing through the long
entrance hall, you come to the building's
focal point (right) – the grand courtyard
and pool, decorated with delicate zellige,
carved cedarwood friezes and arabesque
stucco arches, where the students would
have carried out their ritualistic ablutions.
It is worth ascending to the dormitories
situated on the upper floors. According
to the tour guides, 900 boys once cooked,
ate and slept inside these spartan cells.
Off rue Souk El Khemis

12.30 Jardin Majorelle

French artist Jacques Majorelle arrived in Marrakech in 1919, and these exuberant gardens, framed by his namesake blue, are his glorious legacy. A meander along the terracotta-hued pathways takes you on a dreamy journey past rare plants, such as supersized cacti and palms, and across pretty white lily ponds. The property was rescued from disrepair in 1980 by Pierre Bergé and Yves Saint Laurent. A museum, set in a 1931 villa (above) designed by Paul Sinoir, houses a fine collection of Berber art and jewellery, and a boutique filled with handcrafted gifts, including silver teapots with leather handles. Nearby, the Studio KO-conceived Museé Yves Saint Laurent opens in 2017, displaying haute couture garments, sketches and mood boards.
Rue Yves Saint-Laurent, T 05 24 31 30 47, www.jardinmajorelle.com

14.00 Café Clock

Mike Richardson established this outpost of Café Clock in 2014 (the original is in Fez), set inside a 1950s school. He worked with Danish interior architect Else-Rikke Bruun on the eclectic fit-out, which features cosy alcoves built into the concrete; murals by local talent (opposite) and Swiss artist Ramón Bachmann provide colour. The café is a trailblazer for Marrakech; a youthful, inclusive environment that provides a stage for a mix of musicians, calligraphers and storytellers (*hikayat*). Sustenance is simple and tasty, from camel burgers to salads, such as fig and blue cheese with grilled chicken. Our favourite tables are on the terrace (above). Cooking classes are held on the roof, and begin with a tour of the souks to source produce and spices. *224 derb Chtouka, T 05 24 37 83 67, www.cafeclock.com*

15.30 Palais El Badi

This opulent complex was commissioned in 1578 by Ahmed El Mansour, who hired craftsmen from all over the country and imported about 50 tonnes of marble for the job. The palace's incredible internal riches were legendary, until they were pillaged by Alaouite leader Moulay Ismaïl to help complete his own residence in Meknes. Rambling ruins, with a sunken orange grove and dusky pink ramparts, are all that remain, but they provide an extraordinary outdoor setting for large-scale installations, such as Ghanaian artist El Anatsui's pavilion, draped in metallic 'fabrics' crafted from recycled sardine cans and the like. El Badi is also the temporary home of contemporary photography gallery MMP+ (see p072); a perfect synthesis of ancient and modern. *Ksibat Nhass, www.palais-el-badi.com*

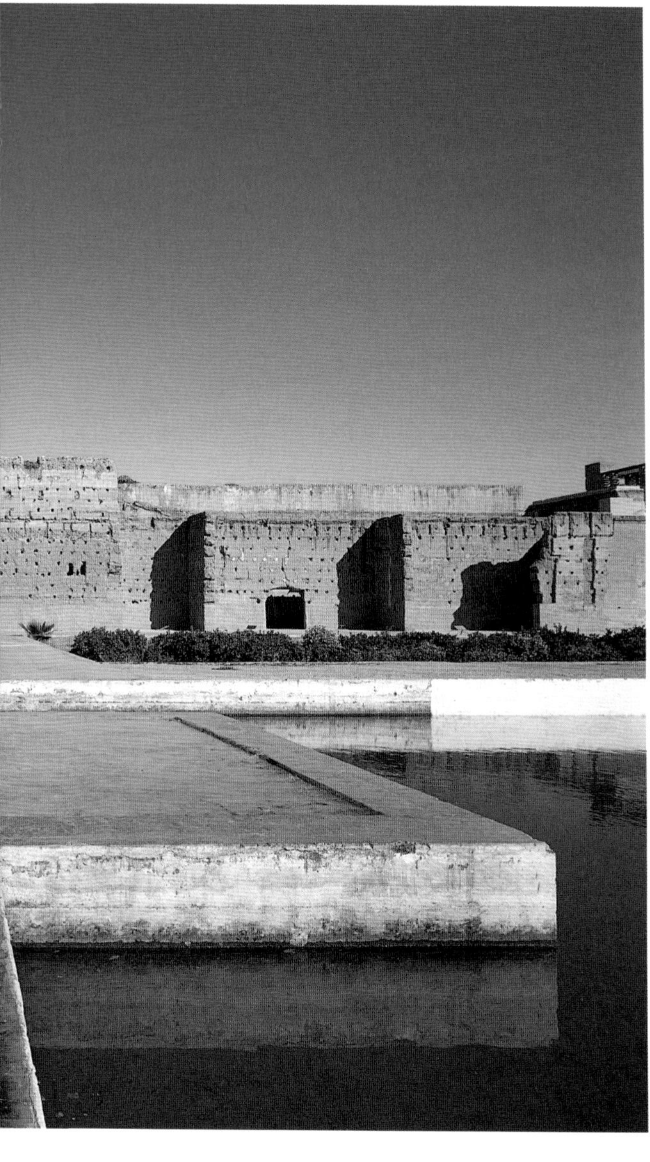

17.00 Royal Mansour Spa

This outsanding spa was designed by the architects OBMI and covers 2,500 sq m. The honeycomb-like structure (opposite) through which guests enter is opulent without being overbearing, and instils an instant sense of calm. The pampering options include two hammams (for men and women) with hot, warm and cold areas, treatments using MarocMaroc, Dr Hauschka or Sisley products, as well as a Chanel Espace Beauté cabin offering six types of facial. For couples, there are private therapy suites. The surrounding gardens, which are dotted with lemon trees, were landscaped by Madrid-based Luis Vallejo, who drew inspiration from the Alhambra in Granada. Admire them while you lounge by the pool (above).
Rue Abou Abbas El Sebti, T 05 29 80 82 00, www.royalmansour.com

19.00 Le 18

Casablanca-born photographer Laila Hida's progressive initiative Le 18 was established in 2013 and has sprouted wings to become the HQ of cultural workshops and multi-faceted artist residencies in the city. It often supports Mahgrebi themes, while the ongoing KawKaw project is a series of talks that foster dialogue between local and international creatives. The typical *dar* in which it is housed has been given a smart makeover, featuring whitewashed walls, arches and columns, and geometric tiling. There is also a small boutique here, run in partnership with Tangier's Librairie des Colonnes, selling lovely art books. Film screenings, co-hosted by the Rabat-based gallery Le Cube, round out the dynamic programme; do check for evening events. *18 derb El Ferrane, T 05 24 38 98 64, www.le18.weebly.com*

20.30 Nomad

When Nomad launched in 2014, it was a breath of fresh air in the somewhat staid medina dining scene. Set in a restored rambling pile, the decor has a late 1950s and early 1960s vibe, when Marrakech fancied itself as a landlocked Saint Tropez, and features a monochrome palette with yellow accents and wool Berber blankets reappropriated as upholstery. The roof terrace (overleaf), decorated with taupe parasols strung with wicker lanterns, has views over the Place des Épices. The menu comprises modern Moroccan dishes such as zucchini and goat's cheese fritters, and a saffron-scented date cake with salted caramel. There's also a sophisticated list of boutique wines; all of which make this one of the most seductive spots in town. *1 derb Aarjan, T 05 24 38 16 09, www.nomadmarrakech.com*

URBAN LIFE

CAFÉS, RESTAURANTS, BARS AND NIGHTCLUBS

In the past few years, the city's nightlife has migrated away from the sensory overload of the medina to the cosmopolitan enclaves of Guéliz and Hivernage. First-time visitors might get a kick out of sipping mint tea while relaxing on a candlelit terrace, or dancing next to a scantily clad local, but the in-crowd frequents a clutch of more sophisticated cocktail bars and clubs. At venues such as the basement jazz haunt Dahab Club and the hip rooftop O'Sky bar at La Renaissance (89 boulevard Zerktouni, T 05 24 33 77 77), local hospitality blends seamlessly with European tastes.

Marrakech's restaurants are modernising too, as an influx of foreign chefs are attracted by the idea of reimagining the national cuisine, which is notoriously heavy. Restaurants like I Limoni (40 rue Diour Saboun, T 05 24 38 30 30), which has a retro dining room and an Italian/Moroccan menu, reflect a more modish side of the medina. In the *ville nouvelle,* eating out has a laidback vibe thanks to a new wave of bistros. Try buzzy Le Loft (18 rue de la Liberté, T 05 24 43 42 16), chilled Amaia (84 avenue Hassan II, T 05 24 45 71 81) and *bar à vin* Le Studio (85 boulevard Moulay Rachid, T 05 24 43 37 00). Fine diners are still uncommon; seek out chef Yannick Alleno's La Grande Table at the Royal Mansour (rue Abou Abbas El Sebti, T 05 29 80 82 82), or try the Royal Palm's Al Aïn (route d'Amizmiz km12, T 05 24 48 78 00), for Arabic-Berber fusion. *For full addresses, see Resources.*

Dar Cherifa

Close to Jemaa El Fna, this splendid art gallery and 'literary café' is housed in an early 16th-century riad, where the original features have been stripped back and allowed to breathe. The owner, Abdellatif Ben Abdallah, is a local cultural doyen and renovator of numerous riads in the medina. Here, he organises exhibitions, readings and music events. Arrive for a light lunch (order the salads – candied tomatoes, slices of courgette marinated in olive oil and lemon juice, and peppery aubergine, to name a few), or some mint tea and pastries. Spend time admiring the architecture and scanning Dar Cherifa's collection of books on Moroccan art and crafts. Be sure to quiz your waitress or waiter for details of upcoming soirées.
8 derb Chorfa Lakhir, T 05 24 42 64 63, www.dar-cherifa.com

Beldi Country Club

This ambrosial pile, set amid rose gardens and acres of olive groves, is a 20-minute drive from the centre and a great escape from the brouhaha of the medina. In the evening, when the grounds are lit up by lanterns, it has provided the backdrop to some of Marrakech's most fabled parties. The complex comprises a rambling pisé hotel and spa, an elegantly curated 'souk' selling pottery and textiles, a greenhouse (above), a conservatory dining area, which serves farm-fresh Moroccan-Med dishes by day, and the stylishly boho restaurant Le Palmier Fou, for a more formal supper. In summer, take advantage of a day pass to camp out on a canvas 'BKF' chair beside the black-tilled pool, and order a simple lunch of grilled sole on the terrace.
Route du Barrage km6, T 05 24 38 39 50, www.beldicountryclub.com

Namazake

The wraparound rooftop terrace at The Pearl (see p016) has proved a stylish addition to the city's restaurant and bar scene, drawing a crowd of fashionable locals and out-of-towners. Accessed by non-hotel guests via a glass lift from the street, the tiered wooden deck, which has a ring-shaped swimming pool at its centre, offers magnificent views of the medina's ramparts (see p012), orange groves, and the Atlas Mountains in the distance. Open-air Japanese restaurant Namazake (above) is impressive too, the light, raw food providing culinary respite from the lunchtime heat. Chilled-out in the day, the atmosphere ramps up after dark when the robata and teppanyaki grills flame and DJs take to the decks.
Avenue Echouhada/rue du Temple, T 05 24 42 42 42, www.thepearlmarrakech.com

Kechmara

It was back in 2004 that brothers Arnaud and Pascal Foltran first opened Kechmara, in a 1950s villa. The glassed-in frontage used to be a scruffy garden and the bar area was a mechanic's garage. They then set up their own factory, now closed, to make reproduction Eero Saarinen 'Tulip' chairs and Verner Panton dining tables, which were combined here with 1950s and 1960s lamps sourced from markets such as Bab El Khemis. The venue was stripped back and updated in 2015 to create a sleek space featuring moss-green and chrome accents. Located in the centre of Guéliz, it is busy at all hours, from morning coffee to lunch on the roof – maybe saffron-infused octopus – and evening beers, when live bands and DJs pep up the atmosphere.
*3 rue de la Liberté, T 05 24 42 25 32,
www.kechmara.com*

Azar
The neo-oriental Azar has kept its cool
factor since 2010. Owners Marcel and
Grégory Chiche, who also run the hip Le
Comptoir Darna (see p062), hired local
designer Younes Duret to create the look.
In the chic restaurant (pictured), sample
Moroccan, Mediterranean or Lebanese
cuisine, then chill out over cocktails and
shisha in the intimate mezzanine club.
Rue de Yougoslavie, T 05 24 43 09 20

Bo-Zin

In the mid-noughties this was about the only place to go for a proper night out. It has some competition now (see p048), but Bo-Zin still has a loyal following among the see-and-be-seen set, particularly at the weekends. Conceived by Studio KO, the design harks back to a time when the city was all tadelakt and crushed velvet. The dining space is warmed by open hearths and dimmed lighting, and art deco-style French doors open out onto the bamboo-hemmed garden, decorated with Bedouin tents. There's a long, somewhat muddled menu that ranges from Japanese dishes to tagines, but the well-preened folk aren't really here to eat; rather, we suggest you sip cocktails, or enjoy the predominantly French wine list, until the small hours.
Route de l'Ourika km3.5, T 05 24 38 80 12, www.bo-zin.com

Riad Yima

The gallery and tearooms of artist Hassan Hajjaj, known in international circles as Morocco's Andy Warhol after his work was exhibited at the V&A in London and the Taymour Grahne Gallery in New York, are a joyous clash of colour, texture and pure pop. Cement tiles in lurid 1970s patterns line the floor, and neon-hued Senegalese plastic woven mats form a backdrop on one wall, framing his iconic 'Kech Angels' series of photographs depicting badass veiled women on scooters who work as henna tattoo artists in the Jemaa El Fna. Drop by to peruse his flour-bag babouche slippers and Moroccan flag pouffes, and stay for sweet mint tea and almond pastries amid lanterns crafted from sardine cans and waxed tarps emblazoned with pattern.
52 derb Aajane, T 06 65 16 75 54, www.riadyima.com

Le Jardin

Marrakechi entrepreneur Kamal Laftimi launched this eaterie, housed in a 16th-century riad, in 2011. He conceived the design with Anne Favier, who wanted to create an urban oasis, incorporating the trees already growing in the courtyard. The venue consists of a library/living room (above), an alfresco dining area (opposite), an upstairs space selling contemporary kaftans by Algerian designer Norya Ayron,

and a rooftop terrace. This is a popular medina hangout, as are Laftimi's other ventures, Nomad (see p045) and Café des Épices (T 05 24 39 17 70). Stop off for lunch while shopping in the souks, or a cool beer. Unusually for this area (and testament to Laftimi's negotiating skills), Le Jardin has a licence to serve alcohol.
32 Souk El Jeld, Sidi Abdelaziz,
T 05 24 37 82 95, www.lejardin.ma

Le Zinc
Several restaurants have opened in Sidi Ghanem over the past few years, with varying success. Le Zinc has been a hit, thanks to French chef Damien Durand. His bistro wouldn't look out of place in the 2nd arrondissement of Paris. Come for lunch and a plate of staunchly Gallic fare, like fish with gratin dauphinois.
517 rue Principale, ZI Sidi Ghanem,
T 05 24 33 59 69

INSIDER'S GUIDE
ARTSI IFRACH, FASHION DESIGNER

At his pint-sized boutique (see p084) in Souk Cherifia (see p080), Artsi Ifrach's eclectic garments combine flamboyant West African prints with leather, velvet and embroidery, Bakelite and costume jewellery. 'This tiny shop expresses my universe,' he says. 'I am obsessed with tradition, which is the key to Marrakech.'

Ifrach lives in the Mellah, the old Jewish quarter, and suggests visitors stay in a riad in the medina, for a more personal experience. He might start his day with breakfast or coffee in the garden at La Mamounia (see p026), which is 'always a delight', and often takes a casual stroll around the Africa Market (behind the Jemaa El Fna Market) for 'rare, locally crafted pieces, like amazing silk scarves, woven bread baskets and beaded statues'. Most days he has lunch at La Famille (42 Riad Zitoun Jdid, T 06 69 04 11 37), which serves organic dishes, such as barley salad with peach, mint and peanuts, and flat bread accompanied by a smoky olive tapenade, within a whitewashed, Mediterranean-style courtyard. 'This restaurant nails the Moroccan concept of *beldi*, which celebrates simplicity.'

To recharge, Ifrach heads for the stylish desert retreat La Pause (Douar Lmih Laroussiene, Agafay, T 06 10 77 22 40). And to blow off steam in town, he dances the night away at Le Comptoir Darna (avenue Echouhada, T 05 24 43 77 02). 'It's lots of fun. It feels like a scene from a movie, with beautiful people and great drinks.'
For full addresses, see Resources.

ART AND DESIGN
GALLERIES, STUDIOS AND PUBLIC SPACES

Classical painting, calligraphy, textiles and ceramics were the only officially recognised art forms in Morocco for centuries, however attitudes changed after the inaugural Biennale in 2004 when the authorities began to take contemporary art seriously. The scene in Marrakech has since grown into one of the most fascinating in North Africa. Alongside a proliferation of high-quality galleries including BCK (rue Ibn Aïcha, Résidence Al Hadika El Koubra, T 05 24 44 93 31), Matisse (61 rue de Yougoslavie, T 05 24 44 83 26), 127 (127 avenue Mohammed V, T 05 24 43 26 67) and Rê (Résidence Al Andalous III, T 05 24 43 22 58) are collaborative enterprises like Le 18 (see p044) and individual projects, notably the riotous Riad Yima (see p057), the domain of the country's most infamous artist. The 2016 Biennale introduced street art (it was previously illegal), featuring giant works such as Hendrik Beikirch's 'Tracing Morocco' portraits, created at Montresso (see p070), and it exploded across the country; David Bloch (see p066) exhibits the best talent.

In design, the Moroccan aesthetic remains lavish and OTT. The most interesting ateliers, including the lighting specialists Henry Cath (139 Sidi Ghanem, T 05 24 33 88 33) and Laurence Landon (see p092), are opening up in the old industrial quarter of Sidi Ghanem. But it's the tiles at Popham (opposite) and the metalwork at Yahya Création (see p068) that are the real treasures in this city.
For full addresses, see Resources.

Popham Design

Caitlin and Samuel Dowe-Sandes created Popham in 2006 after emigrating from the US to renovate a riad. Unable to find tiles with a contemporary design, they created their own, and business is now thriving, with high-profile clients including Soho Beach House in Miami and Halcyon House in New South Wales. The patterns, such as 'Toubkal' (above, from €130 per sq m), which was inspired by the highest peak in the Atlas, can be configured in different ways, and are handmade by artisans using low-impact methods in a small factory 7km outside the centre. Make an appointment to visit the workshop, and then stroll down the path to the showroom, which is set in a beautifully renovated country house that demonstrates the tiles' true potential.
Route de l'Ourika km7, Tassoultante,
T 05 24 37 80 22, www.pophamdesign.com

David Bloch Gallery
Galleries are launching thick and fast in the city but few have as strong a pedigree and ethos as David Bloch. Its focus is on street art, particularly the graphic and abstract ('Hall of Fame IV' group show, pictured), and it represents many of the top names from Europe, the US and Morocco, such as Larbi Cherkaoui and Morran Ben Lahcen.
8 bis, rue des Vieux Marrakchis, T 05 24 45 75 95, www.davidblochgallery.com

Yahya Création

Arguably the city's most prolific and most secretive designer, Yahya Rouach makes furnishings, accessories, artworks and lighting, using materials such as nickel silver, brass, glass and mother-of-pearl, and a filigree-like technique. It was in 2004 that Rouach became fascinated by the beaten metalwork that he witnessed in the souks, and started noting ideas that combined the craft with contemporary forms. Today, he employs about 300 craftsmen to cater for a client list that includes Hollywood A-listers, royals and luxury hotels. Rouach also collaborates with other artists, such as calligrapher Mehdi Qotbi; their work was on show at L'Institut du Monde Arabe in Paris. *49-50 passage Ghandouri, 61 rue de Yougoslavie, T 05 24 42 27 76, www.yahyacreation.com*

Voice Gallery

Italian Rocco Orlacchio opened Voice after the Arab Spring as a platform for artistic comment, seeing Marrakech as a bridge between African and occidental cultures. This is evident in the typically solo shows. Tangier-based sculptor Houda Terjuman used tree roots and nests as a metaphor for exile and the search for belonging, and French-born Moroccan Sara Ouhaddou's project to reinvigorate traditional crafts included encouraging a group of Tétouan embroiderers to work with recycled rubber (instead of silk) to produce contemporary stools. 'Hybridations' (above), by Fez native Abdeljalil Saouli, explored the existential, infusing natural materials with mythical symbolism. Voice also champions young Moroccan talent on the global circuit.
366 Sidi Ghanem, T 05 24 33 67 70, www.voicegallery.net

Montresso Jardin Rouge

This farm was converted into an artists' residency in 2009, and now offers studio space and accommodation for up to six creatives who propose a specific project. The foundation aims to attract collectors and benefactors, and you can book a tour; email contact@montresso.com to make an appointment. A multitude of works are displayed throughout the communal areas, hangar-like exhibition room and grounds, including large-scale installations, as well as graffiti sprayed onto the richly coloured adobe walls. We liked Kouka's portraits of Bantu warriors on wood, Ceet's cartoonish chicken sculptures, photographer Gérard Rancinan's *The Raft of Illusions*, inspired by the classic Théodore Géircault painting, and pieces by JonOne, Fenx, Hendrik Beikirch, Cédrix Crespel and Tarek Benaoum (above). *www.montresso.com*

ARCHITOUR
A GUIDE TO MARRAKECH'S ICONIC BUILDINGS

Arab construction is, by nature, inward-looking and private, and much of Marrakech's eye candy is to be found in the detail. Since the early 1970s, the New Moroccan Style, conceived by architects such as Stuart Church and Charles Boccara, and designer Bill Willis, transformed ruins into stunning palaces for celebrity clients. It was the inspiration for the hotel-riad phenomenon, which has been a saving grace, as many properties were wrecks before the boom. Not only did their renovation rekindle the dying local arts of stucco, mosaic and woodwork, it made residential architecture accessible for the price of a room or a meal. As for an original 18th-century interior, the Musée de Mouassine (see p074) is exceptional.

The new town deserves a renaissance too, and looks as if it might finally be getting one. The Save Cinemas Association, in conjunction with Simon Xavier Guerrand-Hermés, has launched a project to preserve Guéliz's 1920s heritage, including the Ciné Théâtre Palace (rue Yougoslavie) and various villas, to mark the recent centenary. Then there is David Chipperfield's Museum for Photography and Visual Arts (MMP+), which has long been in the pipeline. Situated next to Menara Gardens (see p014), the 6,000 sq m terracotta-hued pisé cube will comprise galleries and terraces set around an atrium. Meanwhile, there's lots to savour in the city's monuments, which tell a dogged history of occupation and outstanding craftsmanship. *For full addresses, see Resources.*

Palais de la Bahia

The most intact and striking of the city's palaces, Bahia oozes imperial grandeur. It was built in two distinct stages. Its original commissioner, the Grand Vizier Si Moussa, oversaw construction from 1859 to 1873, intending it to be the most extraordinary residence of its time. His ultimate success in this endeavour was ensured by his son, Ba Ahmed, who bid to outdo his old man by employing an architect who had worked in Andalusia to design a succession of extra courtyards and wings from 1894 to 1900. There are 160 rooms decorated with acres of hand-cut zellige, painted cedar ceilings inlaid with gold leaf, and intricately carved pink plaster. The harem in particular is a delight – a joyful, exuberant space where bold stripes and floral patterns collide.
5 rue Riad Zitoun El Jdid,
www.palais-bahia.com

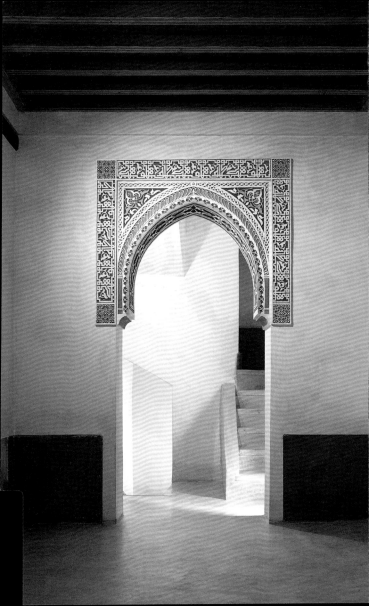

Musée de Mouassine

This late 16th- to early 17th-century *douiria* (the guest annex to a Saadian nobleman's house) was restored by Patrick Manac'h (see p033), with the help of Louvre curator Xavier Salmon, between 2012 and 2014. It is laid out around a square patio with a wood dome and skylight and two alcoves framed by carved cedar mantels. Leading off it is a salon (above), a bedroom and a roof terrace (now a tearoom). The interior is extraordinarily detailed, and features painted ceilings and Kufic script carved into plaster, which is inset with vibrant pigments. Surprisingly bright and airy, it gives a real sense of the opulence of the times, and hosts exhibitions, events and a collection of works by Delacroix, who lived in Morocco from 1831 to 1832.

4-5 derb El Hammam, T 05 24 37 77 92, www.museedemouassine.com

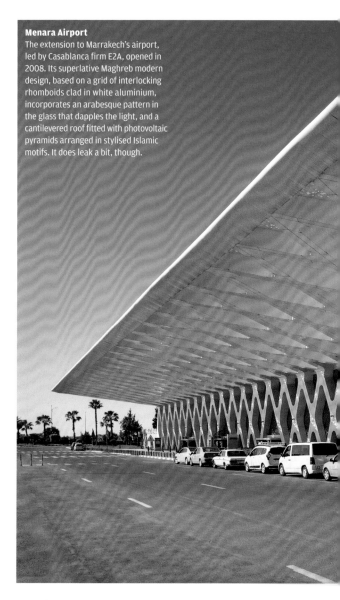

Menara Airport
The extension to Marrakech's airport, led by Casablanca firm E2A, opened in 2008. Its superlative Maghreb modern design, based on a grid of interlocking rhomboids clad in white aluminium, incorporates an arabesque pattern in the glass that dapples the light, and a cantilevered roof fitted with photovoltaic pyramids arranged in stylised Islamic motifs. It does leak a bit, though.

Saadian Tombs

Marrakech's Saadian period (the dynasty ruled Morocco from 1554-1659) has been dubbed its golden age – literally. The Saads had a voracious appetite for gold, and used it in abundance in their palaces and garden pavilions. But if they knew how to live, they knew how to die as well. The Saadian Tombs in the Kasbah district are so exquisite that even the dynasty's conquerors, the Alaouites, chose to leave them intact when ransacking the city. The 66 tombs are distributed over two buildings, with separate rooms for the kings, their wives and children, and a more sombre chamber for servants. The centrepiece is the Hall of Twelve Columns (above), where the tombs' creator, Sultan Ahmed El Mansour, lies beneath a marble tombstone set on a glorious zellige floor.
Rue de la Kasbah

Koubba El Badiyin

Part of the Ben Youssef complex, which includes a mosque and a Koranic school, or *medersa* (see p034), this *koubba* is the only intact relic of the Almoravids' reign in the city (1062-1147). An ornamental dome containing the remains of a holy man, a *koubba* is normally off-limits to visitors, but this one is an exception. Dating from the 12th century, the two-storey structure is most appealing once you get past the ablution basins and excavated rubble. The interior is embellished with delicate floral and star motifs, and calligraphy. The arches and merlons are typical of the Almoravid style, which forms the basis of most traditional Moroccan architecture. Other distinguishing features include the ribs on the dome's exterior, and clever square and octagonal internal support. *Off rue Souk El Khemis, T 05 24 44 18 93*

SHOPS

THE BEST RETAIL THERAPY AND WHAT TO BUY

Everyone will tell you that the best craftsmen come from Fez, but aficionados agree that the best shopping is in Marrakech. Lately, a wave of young Moroccan designers has come to the fore; check out their products at 33 rue Majorelle (see p032), and Galerie du Souk Cherifia (Sidi Abdelaziz, T 06 78 38 22 54) in the medina. Most traditional crafts are executed in tiny workshops north of Jemaa El Fna and the specialist bazaars off Souk Smarine and rue Mouassine. Haggling is expected, and for this you will need sharp bargaining powers – prepare to pay between a half and two-thirds of the starting price. Not everything will translate well back home.

For Beni Ouarain carpets, try Lahandira (Foundouk Namouss, 100 derb Sidi Ishak, T 06 77 42 33 53); Chez les Frères Kassri (3 Souk Dylaouine, T 06 62 40 51 02) sells plain blankets; and La Maison Bahira (Boutique 52, 15 Souk Cherifia, T 05 24 38 63 65) purveys fine table and bed linens. The one-stop shop for oriental products is Mustapha Blaoui (144 Arset Aouzal, T 05 24 38 52 40).

The modern stores, like furniture emporium Maison LAB (44 rue Tarik Bnou Ziad, T 05 24 43 39 36), are in Guéliz, around rue de la Liberté and rue des Vieux Marrakchis. Although the new town is eclipsing the industrial zone as a hunting ground for design, Sidi Ghanem (see p064) is worth a visit. A notable outlet is appointment-only Florence Teillet (T 06 61 22 59 05), for handwoven throws. *For full addresses, see Resources.*

Lalla

Laetitia Trouillet relocated her showroom
to this former white goods shop in Guéliz
in 2015, and it remains *the* pilgrimage
spot for touring buyers, journalists and
fashionistas looking for stylish one-off
items. The space consists of her studio
and a light-filled storefront, which features
handcrafted cement floor tiles, sourced
from the local maker Popham Design (see
p065). Trouillet's cool, cultish handbags
include the oversized, butter-soft 'Kaouki'
leather tote, the fringed 'Hippy Habibi'
suede drawstring bag, and kitschy terry
cloth clutches, which put a modern spin
on ethnic prints. In addition, she invites
local and international designers to stock
their accessories; seek out Parme Marin's
necklaces, studded with bones and beads.
35 boulevard Mansour Eddahbi,
T 05 24 44 72 23, www.lalla.fr

Soufiane

Finding the right carpet in the souks is not easy. Brothers Ismail Mouahid and Soufiane Zarib use traditional motifs as inspiration for contemporary designs, and stock strong offerings from 25 key regions in Morocco. This showroom is set in a handsome Saadian townhouse; the duo opened a second, more modern shopfront in 2016, also in the medina.
13 Souk des Tapis, T 06 15 28 56 90

Art/C

On the first floor of Souk Cherifia, Art/C is the brilliantly quirky showcase of Israeli-Moroccan designer Artsi Ifrach (see p062). It's only a small space, with white walls and cream-and-butter-hued floor tiles, but it really pops. Alongside Ifrach's joyfully exuberant creations, there is a vermillion and hot-pink rug sourced from Azilal in the Atlas Mountains, and a Berber straw hat, festooned with pom-poms, which functions as a light fixture. The artistically rendered, one-off garments transcend trends; the relaxed overcoats, full trousers and decorative dresses feature a witty patchwork of textures and materials, and idiosyncratic detailing, such as Bakelite brooches. There are also clutch bags and boots adorned with tribal-print fabric.
Souk Cherifia, T 06 60 03 62 46, www.art-c-fashion.com

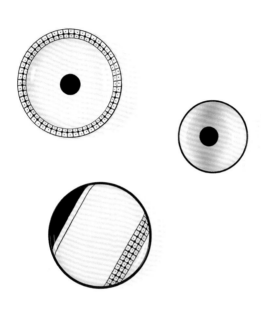

Ewwel

The Tamazight word 'ewwel' translates as dream, and Berber culture and motifs are instrumental in Paris native Sarah Charpentier's designs. She has travelled across Morocco foraging for inspiration, which might come in the form of Tifinagh script, or a decorated door in a remote village. For her line of ceramic tableware, Charpentier nattily reappropriates these traditional elements into clean, modern patterns; the subtly decorative, functional cream-and-black 'Assiettes' line (above, starting from €8) caught our eye, and is produced in a Fez-based pottery studio. Ewwel's offering has since expanded to include cheery notebooks, with cover art that draws on the city's ornamental tiles, and cotton place mats edged with simple, embroidered shapes in primary colours. *www.ewwel-shop.com*

El Fenn Boutique

Opened in 2015, this boutique, housed at the El Fenn hotel (see p016), is co-curated by the erstwhile director of Ford Models Paul Rowland, Alessandra Lippini, formerly of Italian *Vogue*, and Willem Smit, who also conceived the eclectic interiors. A red herringbone tile staircase leads down to a treasure trove of quality, artisan-made wares, and more. Vintage cocktail dresses by Yves Saint Laurent, Chanel and Lanvin grace one rail, Rowland's leather ponchos hang on another, and elsewhere you will find studded bags from Maroc'n Roll, hand-blown glassware by Verre Beldi (T 05 24 38 39 50), embroidered linens and silks by Alnour and coffee table books by Katakali Libraire. The space also hosts exhibitions, and doubles as a lively restaurant and bar.
2 derb Moulay Abdullah Ben Hezzian, T 05 24 44 12 10, www.el-fenn.com

Fenyadi

When three of Sidi Ghanem's prime design businesses – Akkal (ceramics by Charlotte Barkowski), Via Notti (textiles) and Amira Bougies (ornamental candles) – sold their individual concerns in 2010, they decided to come together under one roof as one brand. Fenyadi launched in this converted warehouse in industrial Sidi Ghanem, but after switching its flagship to Casablanca, it relocated to smaller premises down the road in 2015, where the main focus is now on ceramics. The trio come up with a new range each season, coordinating in order to produce a sleek, cohesive collection. A common theme is the Saharan landscape, which inspires a palette of burnt umber, yellow ochre, greens and blues; the wares in navy and dusky pink conjure Marrakech.
315 ZI Sidi Ghanem, T 05 24 33 61 17, www.fenyadi.com

Marrakshi Life

Fashion photographer turned designer Randall Bachner makes unconventional, elegant menswear in high-quality wool, linen and cotton. The range is crafted by four local weavers and six tailors, who work from a light-filled atelier in Guéliz, where traditional Moroccan garb is given contemporary form. Signature pieces include hoodless *djellabas*, super-soft bathrobes with a 1970s feel and hand-woven Oxford shirts (above), €140, and matching boxer shorts featuring a wobbly, pastel-blue stripe. There is also a strong line in accessories, such as scarves and tote bags. Make an appointment to visit the workshop (T 06 76 65 03 73), or simply drop by the sliver of a boutique (opposite), which is cloaked in oblong tonal blue tiles. *Souk Cherifia, T 05 24 38 98 76, www.marrakshi.net*

Atelier Laurence Landon

Laurence Landon established her studio in 2006, to create sumptuous lighting and interior decor pieces – from candlestick holders to bookshelves – that take their cues from Bauhaus and art deco styles. Look out for the smoked glass lanterns at street level, which lead to the first-floor showroom displaying Landon's handsome wares, including a series of black-edged, rounded mirrors that connect to form a playful wall sculpture, lit from behind; a set of chrome-plated bubble lights; and sinuous table lamps, crafted from steel and polished brass. It is also possible to order bespoke items. The custom-made lamps and shimmering mirrored coasters scattered around Peacock Pavilions (see p024) should provide ample inspiration.
294 Zl Sidi Ghanem, T 06 63 72 70 02, www.atelierlandon.com

Chabi Chic

Launched in 2012 by French duo Nadia Noël and Vanessa Di Mino, Chabi Chic injected a dose of modernity and wit into traditional Moroccan craft. The flagship store in Sidi Ghanem has a natty black-and-white facade, which contrasts with a pared-back interior of cement alcoves and simple pine shelving. The range has expanded to include bath accessories, such as hammam towels, woven Sahara storage baskets, organic cosmetics and deli items, including spices, teas, honey and Argan oil. The ceramics are fired in Fez and hand-painted in neat stripes, or with fronds and feathers in soft oranges, purples and greens. More minimal vessels, like cups, bowls and vases, are rendered in white and terracotta; mix and match.
322 Zl Sidi Ghanem, T 05 24 35 65 60, www.chabi-chic.com

Kaftan Queen

Sarah Rouach's boutique in an up-and-coming shopping enclave in Guéliz is a must-visit store for women in search of contemporary Moroccan fashion. Using new and vintage fabrics, and different styles of embroidery – a specialist craft in this country – Rouach produces mostly kaftans and draped dresses. Her clothes combine oriental and Western styles, in elegant modern designs. She has since expanded her range to include decorated *babouches* (the leather slippers you will see on sale all over the medina), belts that are detailed with intricate hand-carved bronze buckles designed by her husband, Yahya Rouach (see p068), silver clutches and leather bags with metallic handles.
41 passage Ghandori, 61 rue de Yougoslavie, T 05 24 42 07 97, www.kaftanqueeneshop.com

ESCAPES

WHERE TO GO IF YOU WANT TO LEAVE TOWN

The happy location of Marrakech, cradled between the mountains and the sea, provides plenty of options for skipping town. Less than an hour away, in the foothills of the Atlas, the Ourika Valley is ideal for a day's hiking. Hotels range from modest *douars* (traditional Berber houses) to more deluxe resorts; Kasbah Bab Ourika (route de l'Ourika, T 06 61 63 42 34) and Kasbah du Toubkal (Imlil, T 05 24 48 56 11) are good choices. Glamp it up at Scarabeo Camp (see p098) or further south-east at Erg Chigaga Luxury Desert Camp (El Gouera, T 06 54 39 85 20), which is a nine-hour drive from Marrakech. For sea air minus the crowds of Essaouira (see p102), those in the know travel to El Jadida and Oualidia on the Atlantic coast. Stay at L'Iglesia hotel (see p103) or, if you are in a group, at Lagoon Lodge (R301 km4, www.lagoonlodgemorocco.com), which overlooks Oualidia's beautiful waters from its infinity pool.

In northern Morocco, once bohemian Tangier is undergoing a renaissance. Villas of Morocco (T 05 22 36 12 12) has a range of chic private rentals, or try Hotel Nord-Pinus (11 rue du Riad Sultan, T 06 61 22 81 40) in the kasbah. Fez (opposite) has one of the oldest and best-preserved medinas in the Arab world. It is arguably more captivating than Marrakech's and not as frenetic. From here, take a day trip to the Roman city of Volubilis, north of Meknes. It might be less well known than Pompeii, but it's no less splendid.
For full addresses, see Resources.

Fez

A seven-hour train ride from Marrakech, Fez has some of Islam's most significant buildings, including the vast 9th-century Karaouine Mosque, and the glorious shrine of Moulay Idriss II. Enter the medina at Bab Boujloud to step back in time. There are no cars and few mopeds, just a riveting stream of humanity. Contemporary ventures are now making their mark – Karawan Riad (T 05 35 63 78 78) here, as well as Hotel Sahrai (T 05 35 94 03 32) in the new town, are game-changers in a place so deeply traditional, while the restaurant Numéro 7 (above; T 06 94 27 78 49), designed by Stephen di Renza, is a stage for roving chefs on two- to four-month residencies. Head to The Ruined Garden at Riad Idrissy (T 06 49 19 14 10) for updated Fassi streetfood, and Palais Faraj's crow's-nest bar (T 05 35 63 53 56) for a sundowner with a view.

Scarabeo Camp, Agafay

In the isolated hills of the Agafay region, 40km from Marrakech, Vincent T'Sas and Florence Mottet's desert retreat, which is named after a beetle native to the area, is a contemporary take on the nomadic camp. Yet the accommodation is far from rustic: billowing white tents house beds fashioned from lemon-tree wood, duvets and cotton linen, African woven matting, Berber rugs, local artwork, Moroccan lanterns and en-suite eco-bathrooms. The food is superb, as is the range of activities offered, from hiking to nearby villages to quad-biking, star-gazing with a local astronomer and hot-air ballooning. However, many guests are content simply to sit and contemplate the fluctuating light of this awe-inspiring landscape. A sister settlement on the coast (T 06 62 80 08 23) launched in 2016.
T 06 61 44 41 58, www.scarabeocamp.com

L'Amandier, Ouirgane Valley
In the foothills of the Atlas, this elegant
boutique retreat opened in 2016. British
brothers Anwar and Riaz Harland-Khan
worked with architects Nick Gowing and
Michael Kopinski on the interiors, which
feature plenty of terracotta, marble and
stone, embellished by accents of turquoise
and gold. There is a series of suites and
villas, the latter with a sleek, well-equipped
kitchen, private plunge pool (above) and
spacious roof terrace with cabanas and
panoramic views. L'Amandier is a one-hour
trip by car from Marrakech, through olive
and citrus groves. Adjust to the change
of pace with a sundowner beside the 25m
tadelakt-tiled infinity pool. From here,
there's a superlative vista of lush valleys,
red-earth hills and distant peaks. This is a
good base from which to head out skiing
in season (from December to March).
L'Amandier Plateau, T + 44 207 754 5563,
www.lamandierhotel.com

Essaouira

Two hours' drive west through the desert to the coast, whitewashed Essaouira is the antithesis of Marrakech – laidback and devoid of *le jet*-type decadence (for now). The Portuguese built a fortress here in the early 16th century, but the city dates to two centuries later when the Alaouite sultan ordered French architect Théodore Cornut to devise a modern grid-like layout. Orson Welles shot scenes for his 1952 film version of *Othello* in Essaouira and it has hosted many artists and musicians; Bob Marley and Jimi Hendrix loved the place, and the renowned Gnaoua music festival is held in June (www.festival-gnaoua.net). The riad offerings continue to evolve. The villa Dar Beida (above; T 06 67 96 53 86) combines white-walled cool with Moroccan and retro furnishings, as does Riad Dar Maya (T 05 24 78 56 87), which has a rooftop hot tub.

El Jadida and Oualidia

These two small Atlantic towns, about four hours' drive from Marrakech, are a well-kept secret. Stretched out along a wide bay, El Jadida's new town has magnificent, if crumbling, art deco architecture, but the real treasures lie within the Portuguese medina. There are five stately churches, and an ancient vaulted water cistern that creates intricate light reflections. Stay at L'Iglesia (above; T 05 23 37 34 00), which occupies the old American consulate and a 19th-century Spanish Catholic church. Sip a gin and tonic in the salon while admiring the capacious proportions of the former nave, now nicely furnished with 'Barcelona' chairs. En route back to Marrakech, take the coastal road south to pretty Oualidia, where you can feast on oysters, lobster and sea bream baked in salt on the terrace of La Sultana hotel (T 05 23 36 65 95).

NOTES

SKETCHES AND MEMOS

RESOURCES

CITY GUIDE DIRECTORY

A

Al Aïn 048
Royal Palm
Route d'Amizmiz km12
T 05 24 48 78 00
www.royalpalm-hotels.com

Amaia 048
84 avenue Hassan II
T 05 24 45 71 81

Art/C 084
Souk Cherifia
T 06 60 03 62 46
www.art-c-fashion.com

Atelier Laurence Landon 093
294 ZI Sidi Ghanem
T 06 63 72 70 02
www.atelierlandon.com

Azar 054
Rue de Yougoslavie
T 05 24 43 09 20
www.azar-marrakech.com

B

BCK Art Gallery 064
Rue Ibn Aïcha
Résidence Al Hadika El Koubra
T 05 24 44 93 31
www.bck.ma

Beldi Country Club 050
Route du Barrage km6
T 05 24 38 39 50
www.beldicountryclub.com

Ben Youssef Medersa 034
Off rue Souk El Khemis

Bo-Zin 056
Route de l'Ourika km3.5
T 05 24 38 80 12
www.bo-zin.com

C

Café Clock 038
224 derb Chtouka
T 05 24 37 83 67
www.cafeclock.com

Café des Épices 059
75 place Rahba Lakdima
T 05 24 39 17 70
www.cafedesepices.net

Chabi Chic 094
322 ZI Sidi Ghanem
T 05 24 35 65 60
www.chabi-chic.com

Chez les Frères Kassri 080
3 Souk Dylaouine
T 06 62 40 51 02
www.bazarkassri.com

Le Comptoir Darna 062
Avenue Echouhada
T 05 24 43 77 02
www.comptoirmarrakech.com

D

Dahab Club 048
La Renaissance
89 boulevard Zerktouni
T 05 24 33 77 77
www.renaissance-hotel-marrakech.com

Dar Cherifa 049
8 derb Chorfa Lakhir
T 05 24 42 64 63
www.dar-cherifa.com

David Bloch Gallery 066
8 bis
Rue des Vieux Marrakchis
T 05 24 45 75 95
www.davidblochgallery.com

HOTELS

ADDRESSES AND ROOM RATES

L'Amandier 100
Room rates:
double, from €210;
Villa, from €350
L'Amandier Plateau
Ouirgane Valley
T +44 207 754 5563
www.lamandierhotel.com

Amanjena 016
Room rates:
double, from €690
Route de Ouarzazate km12
T 05 24 39 90 00
www.aman.com

Bab Hotel 016
Room rates:
double, from €95
Angle boulevard Mansour Eddahbi/rue
Mohamed El Beqqal
T 05 24 43 52 50
www.babhotelmarrakech.ma

Dar Beida 102
Room rates:
house, from €390 per week
Essaouira
T 06 67 96 53 86
www.castlesinthesand.com

Dar Kawa 028
Room rates:
double, from €100;
Olmassi Suite, from €150
18 derb El Ouali
Kaat Ben Nahed
T 06 61 34 43 33
www.darkawa.net

Dar Sabra 016
Room rates:
double, from €95
Douar Abiad
T 05 24 32 91 72
www.darsabra-marrakech.net

El Fenn 016
Room rates:
double, from €300
2 derb Moullay Abdullah Ben Hezzian
T 05 24 44 12 10
www.el-fenn.com

Erg Chigaga Luxury Desert Camp 096
Room rates:
tent, €235 per night
(per person; two-night minimum stay)
Erg Chigaga
El Gouera
T 06 54 39 85 20
www.desertcampmorocco.com

Fellah Hotel 030
Room rates:
double, from €90;
Suite 103, from €170
Route de l'Ourika km13
T 05 25 06 50 00
www.fellah-hotel.com

L'Iglesia 103
Room rates:
double, from €140
El Jadida
T 05 23 37 34 00
www.liglesia.com

Karawan Riad 097
  Room rates:
  double, from €210
  21 derb Ourbia
  Fez
  T 05 35 63 78 78
  www.karawanriad.com
Kasbah Bab Ourika 096
  Room rates:
  double, from €150
  Route de l'Ourika
  Ourika
  T 06 61 63 42 34
  www.kasbahbabourika.com
Kasbah du Toubkal 096
  Room rates:
  double, €170
  Imlil
  T 05 24 48 56 11
  www.kasbahdutoubkal.com
Lagoon Lodge 096
  Room rates:
  double, €210 per night
  (three-night three-room minimum stay);
  riad, €3,500 per week
  R301 km4
  Oualidia
  www.lagoonlodgemorocco.com
La Mamounia 026
  Room rates:
  double, from €410
  Avenue Bab Jdid
  T 05 24 38 86 00
  www.mamounia.com

Mandarin Oriental 018
  Room rates:
  Atlas Suite, from €650
  Route Golf Royal
  T 05 24 29 88 88
  www.mandarinoriental.com/marrakech
Hotel Nord-Pinus 096
  Room rates:
  double, from €190
  11 rue du Riad Sultan
  Tangier
  T 06 61 22 81 40
  www.nord-pinus-tanger.com
Palais Namaskar 022
  Room rates:
  double, from €490;
  Pool Villa, €1,200
  88/69 route de Bab Atlas
  T 05 24 29 98 00
  www.palaisnamaskar.com
Peacock Pavilions 024
  Room rates:
  Atlas Pavilion, €275
  Route de Ouarzazate km18
  T 05 24 48 46 17
  www.peacockpavilions.com
The Pearl 016
  Room rates:
  double, from €500
  Avenue Echouhada/rue du Temple
  T 05 24 42 42 42
  www.thepearlmarrakech.com

P'tit Habibi 016
Room rates:
double, from €125
59 bis Zaouia Sidi Bellabes
T 05 24 37 88 87
www.ptithabibi.com

Riad Dar Maya 102
Room rates:
double, from €120
33 rue d'Oujda
Essaouira
T 05 24 78 56 87
www.riaddarmaya.com

Riad Due 029
Room rates:
double, from €140;
Zan Suite, from €205
2 derb Chentouf
T 05 24 38 76 29
www.riadliving.com

Riad 72 029
Room rates:
double, from €120
72 Arset Awsel
T 05 24 38 76 29
www.riadliving.com

Riad Dixneuf la Ksour 025
Room rates:
Tanger Room, €120;
double, from €155;
Medersa Suite, €190
19 rue Sidi El Yamani
T 05 24 38 41 32
www.dixneuf-la-ksour.com

Riad Elisa 016
Room rates:
double, from €250
21 rue Sidi El Yamani
T 05 24 39 10 22
www.riad-elisa.com

Riad Goloboy 016
Room rates:
double, from €75
94 derb Mbarek
T 06 61 23 03 05
www.riadgoloboy.com

Riad Mena 017
Room rates:
double, from €175;
Traveller suite, €250;
Eileen Gray suite, €300
70 derb Jdid
T 05 24 38 18 28
www.riadmenaandbeyond.com

Riad de Tarabel 016
Room rates:
double, from €210
8 derb Sraghna
T 05 24 39 17 06
www.riad-de-tarabel.com

Hotel Sahrai 097
Room rates:
double, from €200
Bab Lghoul
Dhar El Mehraz
Fez
T 05 35 94 03 32
www.hotelsahrai.com

Scarabeo Camp 098
  Room rates:
  prices on request
  Agafay
  T 06 61 44 41 58
  Atlantic coast
  T 06 62 80 08 23
  www.scarabeocamp.com
Selman 016
  Room rates:
  double, from €390
  Route d'Amizmiz km5
  T 05 24 45 96 00
  www.selman-marrakech.com
Villa Makassar 020
  Room rates:
  double, from €220;
  Suite Grand Luxe Double, €550
  20 derb Chtouka
  T 05 24 39 19 26
  www.villamakassar.com
Villas of Morroco 096
  Room rates:
  prices on request
  Tangier
  T 05 22 36 12 12
  www.villasofmorocco.com

WALLPAPER* CITY GUIDES

Executive Editor
Jeremy Case

Author
Tara Stevens

Art Editor
Eriko Shimazaki

Photography Editor
Rebecca Moldenhauer

Sub-Editor
Belle Place

Junior Editor
Emilee Jane Tombs

Contributor
Sylvia Ugga

Interns
Georgie Emery
Catalina L Imizcoz
Zoe Wagner

Photo/Digital Assistant
Jade R Arroyo

Production Controller
Nick Seston

Wallpaper*® is a
registered trademark
of Time Inc (UK)

First published 2007
Revised and updated
2010, 2012 and 2013
Fifth edition 2016

© Phaidon Press Limited

All prices and venue
information are correct at
time of going to press,
but are subject to change.

Original Design
Loran Stosskopf
Map Illustrator
Russell Bell

Contacts
wcg@phaidon.com
@wallpaperguides

More City Guides
www.phaidon.com/travel

**Marketing & Bespoke
Projects Manager**
Nabil Butt

Phaidon Press Limited
Regent's Wharf
All Saints Street
London N1 9PA

Phaidon Press Inc
65 Bleecker Street
New York, NY 10012

Phaidon® is a registered
trademark of Phaidon
Press Limited

www.phaidon.com

A CIP Catalogue record for
this book is available from
the British Library.

Printed in China

ISBN 978 0 7148 7240 7

PHOTOGRAPHERS

Roger Casas
Mandarin Oriental,
pp018-019
Peacock Pavilions, p024
Riad Dixneuf la Ksour,
p025
Ben Youssef Medersa,
pp034-035
Café Clock, p038, p039
Palais El Badi, pp040-041
Le 18, p044
Nomad, p045, pp046-047
Bo-Zin, p056
Riad Yima, p057
Artsi Ifrach, p063
Voice Gallery, p069
Montresso Jardin Rouge,
p070, p071
Palais de la Bahia, p073
Musée de Mouassine,
p074, p075
Menara Airport, pp076-77
Lalla, p081
Art/C, p084
El Fenn Boutique,
p086, p087
Marrakshi Life, p090
Atelier Laurence Landon,
pp092-093
Chabi Chic, p094

Milo Keller
Koutoubia Mosque,
pp010-011
Ramparts, pp012-013
Dar Cherifa, p049
Saadian Tombs, p078
Koubba El Badiyin, p079

Nagib Khazaka
Menara Gardens,
pp014-015
Villa Makassar, pp020-021
Palais Namaskar,
p022, p023
Dar Kawa, p028
Fellah Hotel, pp030-031
Royal Mansour Spa,
p042, p043
Namazake, p052
Le Jardin, p058, p059
Le Zinc, pp060-061
David Bloch Gallery,
pp066-067
Yahya Création, p068
Soufiane, pp082-083
Fenyadi, pp088-089
Kaftan Queen, p095

Sven Laurent
Scarabeo Camp,
pp098-099

Pete Navey
Beldi Country Club,
p050, p051

Peartree Digital
Ewwel, p085

Richard Powers
Riad Mena, p017

James Reeve
Riad Due, p029
Maison de la
Photographie, p033
Azar, pp054-055

Jean-Michel Ruiz
Marrakech city view,
inside front cover

MARRAKECH

A COLOUR-CODED GUIDE TO THE HOT 'HOODS

SOUTH MEDINA
Overrun with tourists and swerving mopeds, but unmissable for a taste of the old city

PALMERAIE
Luxury resorts and spas are hidden amid the palm trees of this tranquil desert oasis

NORTH MEDINA
Beyond the fascinating souks and Ben Youssef complex, explore a quieter Marrakech

HIVERNAGE
This tree-lined quarter is fast developing a sophisticated hotel and nightlife scene

MELLAH/KASBAH
The most interesting part of the old city, for its architectural mix and majestic monuments

GUÉLIZ
Shops, cafés, restaurants and nightclubs – here you'll find Marrakech at its most urbane

For a full description of each neighbourhood, see the Introduction.
Featured venues are colour-coded, according to the district in which they are located.